My Life with Dylan Thomas

Tony Curtis – recent publications

Crossing Over, Seren, 2007

After the First Death: An Anthology of Wales and War in the Twentieth Century (editor) Seren, 2007

Wales at War: Critical Essays on Literature and Art (editor) Seren, 2007

The Meaning of Apricot Sponge: Selected Writings of John Tripp (editor) Parthian Books, 2010

Eight Pegs, a poetry pamphlet with illustrations by Rozanne Hawksley, Mulfran Press, 2011

Tokens for the Foundlings (editor) Seren, 2012 a charity anthology for the Foundlings Museum in Bloomsbury

Real South Pembrokeshire, Seren, 2011

Common Sense new paintings, music and poetry, with Grahame Davies, Gigi Jones and Mervyn Burtch booklet and DVD from www.commonsensewales.co.uk

Alchemy of Water / Alcemi Dwr poems by Tony Curtis & Grahame Davies photographs by Mari Lloyd-Owen & Carl Ryan Gomer, 2013

My Life with Dylan Thomas

by Tony Curtis

To Bernard
and Val,
with best wishes,

Tony

MULFRAN PRESS

Published March 2014 by Mulfran Press
2 Aber Street, Cardiff CF11 7AG, UK
www.mulfran.co.uk

ISBN 978-1-907327-21-6

Thanks to Margaret, as always my first reader.

In memory of two Swansea University men of letters who passed on while this was being written:

Dr Jim Davies, Dylan Thomas expert

Nigel Jenkins, poet and critic.

On the first day of Dylan's centenary year I called in at his regular watering-hole The Boar's Head in Carmarthen. There would surely be a plaque, possibly details of a Dylan-themed weekend. The bar-man stared blankly back at me as I asked about Dylan and what they had planned. Nothing.

"It's Felinfoel brewery that owns it," he said.

"I think they might be missing a trick," I said.

"Can I get you anything?" he said.

I walked out into Lammas Street: Dark Gate to the right and directly across the road the English Baptist Church's four-column Corinthian portico loomed behind its narrow iron-railing gates. Augustus John punched Dylan Thomas right here, between alcoholic oblivion and the bible-bound gaze of the Lord's people. Then, leaving the roaring boy flat on his back in the road, he bundled Caitlin into his car and, having his wicked way with the gear-box, drove off into the sunset towards Laugharne.

⁂

I had four years at Swansea University when it was called the University College of Swansea, going up in the autumn of 1965: a degree in English and a PGCE year. Plenty of exposure to Dylan Thomas then. Well, no. Thomas was not mentioned by our lecturers, even on the Modern British and American course for which I'd opted. He'd died thirteen years before, so perhaps it was all a bit raw; Kingsley Amis had just left the staff and, no doubt, they'd had too much of larger-than-life writers. Though the English Society did have a steady trickle of fascinating guests – the Irish poet W.R. Rogers, the suave and seductive Dannie Abse, that breaker of fiction boundaries B.S. Johnson (I still have his unbound and to-be-shuffled novel-in-a-box *The Unfortunates* in my glass bookcase); then there were several visits by the poet Jon Silkin, who would hawk the latest issue of his magazine *Stand* around the refectory's tables and lunch-times (he must have come to read three times, at least – it was said later that he was playing Cats and Dogs near the Mermaid Mumbles with a post-grad woman).

There was also a reading by Katherine Raine, another poet invited to do a reading tour of America by John Malcolm Brinnin, though hardly in the staggering steps of Dylan: she was impressively mystifying and spoke of only recognising "true poets" such as Vernon. She was the guest of Vernon Watkins who, in the academic year 1966/67 had been invited to the university as Gulbenkian Fellow. Recently retired as "the oldest bank clerk in Wales; my father was the youngest bank manager" he was assigned to our Modern British and American Literature course, having ticked off two of the three requirements in the mind of Professor Price (Cecil Price always appeared in a gown and was fully occupied, for decades, in editing the letters of Sheridan). The trouble was that Vernon, while obviously not American, by birth or inclination, was also problematically British and certainly not Modern. He declared that he could never write a poem that was "dominated by time"; in his poetry world there could be nothing modern, only ancient truths. Kathleen Raine said that, "with certainty, he walked on holy ground."

The group of ten or so rapidly fell away from our allotted weekly sessions: Vernon Watkins was not a natural teacher of groups and it was difficult to see how what he was going on about would impinge on the end of year exams we were to take. Some weeks it was a girl and me, and some weeks just me. The small poet-buds were in me, though I dared not give any indication of this to the Gulbenkian Fellow and felt honoured to sit at his feet, or on the same bench on campus or in Singleton Park.

This was so long ago and, in truth, I remember little of what was said: except that here was a Faber poet, someone who had signed the petition with T.S. Eliot to plead for the traitorous Ezra Pound's life to be spared; the close friend of Dylan Thomas – they had shared drafts of poems with each other, made suggestions and corrections to each other's work – for whose wedding in 1944 Dylan had not showed up. Bad; but doubly bad because Dylan had agreed to be his best man.

I certainly had no confidence to show

Vernon Watkins my poems. Years later I learned that John Ormond had done this when he was an undergraduate at Swansea: the strictures and precise critiquing of his work were so severe that John was shaken from his course as a poet for some years: "Don't publish anything until you are thirty," Vernon said. What would Vernon Watkins have made of my student scribblings? I'd had a narrow escape. I do remember Watkins talking with insight and enthusiasm about Wilfred Owen; and on the one occasion that I asked him about Dylan Thomas he announced that, "Dylan, of course, was a Christian poet."

In an interview with George Thomas broadcast on BBC radio in February that year Vernon Watkins said, "I find [the students] very interesting. I can't say how good I am as a teacher. All I can say is that I think I learn a lot from doing it. How much they learn is anyone's guess." Well learning comes in many ways and I was, though uncomprehending, gripped by his every word.

My last memory of Vernon Watkins was seeing him on one of the college's tennis courts:

he was still a wiry, athletic man into his sixties, quite the antithesis to podgy, chain-smoking, beer-drinking Dylan. Though just as Dylan had died in America, so would Vernon Watkins later in that autumn, 1966. He had gone on from Swansea to a year as visiting professor in Washington, Seattle, on the recommendation of the recently-departed Theodore Roethke. That August while I was working shifts in the Sunblest bread factory in Saltney in north Wales Vernon, against his doctor's advice, continued to play tennis and had a heart attack. Dylan dead from a succession of whiskies and medical blunders; Vernon dead from too much sport.

Early in the first term of the 1966/67 year a memorial meeting was held on campus which I attended. Years later I wondered whether Ceri Richards had been there; he'd certainly written with great appreciation of his friend. We have a small "Black Swan Elegy for Vernon Watkins" work on paper by the artist in our front room. In the same vein as the large canvas in the Glynn Vivian, it hangs close to two of the original paintings for what became the *Dylan Thomas Suite* of lithographs.

When we were at college of course I took Margaret down to meet my Gran in Pentrefelin Street, Carmarthen. She was welcoming and fed two hungry students with a full roast and pudding. Did she remember anything of Dylan Thomas and his times in the town?

"Well, what I do know is that wife of his, Caitlin, was no better than she should have been."

I was born in Gran's house on Boxing Day, 1946. That year was a good one for Dylan with the appearance of *Deaths and Entrances* in February. Dent printed 3,000 copies as the first edition. Also, in 1946 there were no fewer than fifty-two broadcasts and recordings for the BBC. On the first full day of my life, on the 27th of December he read "The Crumbs of one Man's Year" as the "Today's Talk" following the evening news: twenty guineas. His broadcast and recording earnings alone for 1946 then came to over six hundred and twenty guineas. Not pounds, mind, guineas; that's what a proper poet should be paid. I'm almost certain that my mother, father and grandmother would not have been listening. I had been a breech birth and both I and my mother were lucky to survive, thanks to Nurse Evans, who had been sent for, to come to the house on Boxing Day, mind. *Wara teg*.

In truth "The Crumbs of One Man's Year" was an accurate description of a pot-boiler of a piece – "Dylan Thomas doing a very good and slightly malicious imitation of himself," wrote Martin Armstrong in *The Listener*. If those in Number 50, Pentrefelin Street, had heard Dylan say, "Of what is coming in the New Year I know nothing, except that all that is certain will come like thunderclaps or like comets in the shape of four-leaved clovers," would they have had a premonition that my grandfather in Lancashire was dying, that my mother would have to take the train from Carmarthen, leave me to see him and be stuck up there for weeks in the worst snowfall and big freeze in living memory? That I would be Granny-reared for the first three months of my life? And that I am still trying to work out what that meant.

I had three years at "The Gram", The Queen Elizabeth Grammar School for Boys, before we moved down to Pembrokeshire. I have described those who taught us as

Those well-remembered, rarely-composed men, our masters,
Coloured in our formative years, the clever bastards.

That included our art master, Ken Etheridge:

Ethy the Art taught us nothing at all. Smutty Michaelangeloes, we'd draw in his David's classical balls

And rather die than meet him behind the board –
Hands on flies, backs to the wall.

Ken Etheridge was just one of the dozens, possibly hundreds, of poets who composed elegies to Dylan:

[Dylan] raked the cauldron of Ceridwen and tasted again
The precious drops of inspiration…

More likely the drops of inspiration were Buckley's Bitter in the many and farmer-fuelled pubs across that market town.

∾

From 1969 in my first two years as a teacher at Wilmslow Boys Grammar School in Cheshire I was the reviews editor at a small magazine run from Liverpool by a Swansea university contemporary of ours. I was sent copies of the Peterloo *Phoenix Pamphlet Poets* series which had included Seamus Heaney, Derek Mahon and Michael Longley. It was an indication of the enthusiasm and energy of the editor Harry Chambers that he would bother to send review copies to an obscure small magazine with a readership you could have counted on both hands and feet. Not only that, but he wrote later to thank me for my warm review. Within weeks I had followed up by posting him a selection of my poems and had been accepted as the eighteenth and final Phoenix Pamphlet Poet. My booklet, soft and hard-back, appeared in 1971: it was called *Walk Down a Welsh Wind* and in one of the poems,

An old rum of a seagull bunches his neck,
Buff-feathered into his shuffling body
Muffled round with cold, as he picks
Along the curling line of water.

Noisy echoes indeed.

When I recently Googled this title it was available for £94 from a dealer in Southend; and from an American seller at $15.

ຂ

While teaching in Cheshire Margaret and I started a series of literary evenings in a pub, The George and Dragon in Northwich – with the support of the North West Arts Association: it had a starry guest list – John Arden, Tony Connor, George Macbeth the presenter of the BBC's Poetry Now with that purring Scottish/Oxford accent, a wavy-haired young novelist Melvin Bragg and John Pudney. I'd always been moved by Pudney's short war poem "For Johnny". This man wrote and edited over fifty books, thirteen in the war alone, but was destined to be best remembered for those twelve lines which began:

Do not despair
For Johnny-head-in-air;

This featured in the 1945 film *The Way to the Stars*, spoken by Michael Redgrave.

John Pudney had stood for parliament as a Labour candidate and had married the daughter of A.P. Herbert, an Independent MP. He'd been a school friend of W.H. Auden and Benjamin Britten's at Gresham's School.

None of this I knew, but he had a meal with us before the reading and talked about his friend Dylan Thomas. They'd both been part of literary London from the late 1930s and in 1942 A.P. Herbert, persuaded by John Pudney, had supported Dylan and Caitlin by letting them live in one of two houses he owned in Chiswick. One of the stories we heard concerned Dylan's dress code. It was not unknown for Dylan to wash up at someone's flat after a heavy night and this happened to Pudney several times. Late one morning he returned to find Dylan eventually gone, along with a shirt and a pair of John's best trousers. That afternoon he spotted Dylan holding forth with cronies in the Café Royale. John approached and waited for an opportunity to have a quiet word about the trousers.

"Er, Dylan, perhaps... If I could just have... You see..."

"What?"

"The trousers... my trousers..."

"Eh?"

"Well, I think that, possibly a mistake has... You may be wearing my trousers, Dylan."

At which point the roaring boy drew himself up to his five foot six "above average height for a Welshman" and started unbuttoning: "Do you want them now?" he bellowed. John Pudney quietly withdrew.

Dylan's dress code: when yours wear out or become too dirty – take someone else's.

⁊

The first poetry record I bought was a Caedmon EP of Dylan reading a selection of the work of others, including "To Lizbe Brown" by Thomas Hardy, "Master and Bosun's Song" by Auden and "The Naming of Parts" by Henry Reed, that wonderful poem of rifle drill in the army with Dylan doing a mockney accent for his American audience. Of course, Dylan spent more time and ink in the Second World War desperately trying to avoid conscription than he did on writing poems. I played these poems in my bed-sit in a street just above St Helen's rugby and cricket ground but – and how strange this strikes me now – I never walked up the hill above the town and across to Cwmdonkin Park. Not then, nor at any other time in the four university years I had there. Dylan's park where, who knows, in 1968 there would still have been a park-keeper and – who knows – a hunchback?

In that summer Gary Sobers hit six sixes against Glamorgan on that St Helen's ground; I didn't walk down to see that either. Though Dylan, had he lived, might well have been there; he was a keen cricket watcher when he had the time and certainly saw matches at St Helen's and at Lord's and the Oval.

~

Dylan Thomas was one of the first popular poets of the broadcast and recording age. He gave numerous talks and readings on the BBC and featured in recordings of others' work, including Vernon Watkins's *Ballad of the Mari Llwyd*, in which he performed the Leader of the Dead. He even appeared on BBC TV, in a programme in April, 1953, with Wynford Vaughan-Thomas, Dan Jones, Fred Janes and Vernon Watkins; but as with so many treasures of those early days the TV tape and the *Mari Llwyd* recording were both wiped for re-use. As for the television programme, perhaps that was for the best as Vernon later said that, "Dylan couldn't quite remember his words."

Of course, we have the Caedmon Records recordings and two young American students, Barbara Holdridge and Marianne Mantell, to thank for those. The records they produced have not only provided a steady income for the

Dylan Thomas estate, but it was Holdridge and Mantell, not the Swansea council, who paid for the memorial stone to Dylan by Ronald Cour in Cwmdonkin Park in 1963.

∾

The first work by Ceri Richards I bought was the 1971 Kelpra Press screen-print "Origin of Species" which clearly references his "Crooked Rose" from the *Dylan Thomas Suite* and the great "Black Apple of Gower". I think I sold a signed first edition R.S. Thomas to help cover the cost: *Stones of the Field* first appeared from the Druid Press in Carmarthen, the year that I first appeared at Number 50, Pentrefelin Street: 1946.

Much of Ceri Richards's work after the war and especially in the decade following the death of Dylan Thomas was influenced by, driven by, the poet and his metaphors. Though Ceri had been a Trustee of the Tate Gallery on a board which included T.S. Eliot, it was the roaring, allusive and mystical boyo whose poems moved him to paintings, not the high

Anglican, allusive, mystical man. When Ceri read of Dylan's collapse and hospitalisation he went out and bought another three copies of the *Collected Poems*. These four copies he began to illuminate with pen and ink, most pages, most of the poems. I have the Enitharmon Press facsimile version drawn from these works: three copies are extant, one missing. This is the holy grail for Richards and Dylan collectors: the editor Richard Burns traced it to a Lucille Frost, a friend of the artist and a patient of Gustav Jung's; Jung owned an "Apple of Gower" mandala work in which he saw the essence of much of his own thinking about myths and symbols. But there is no further record of the missing book.

❧

On May 14th 1991 I got a call from the Welsh Academy of Writers: Lawrence Ferlinghetti had come to Cardiff and wanted to visit Dylan's Boat House: would I take him down and look after him for the day?

I picked him up in Cathedral Road in

Cardiff; he had as his companion a foxy red-head, somewhere in her prime. At the Boat House he left me on the path to the writing shed with a view of the estuary and the town and the foxy lady. We admired the view and spotted what could have been a heron. Lawrence returned with a note-book: it was obvious that he'd written a poem.

Back at the B&B in Cathedral Road I interviewed Felinghetti and later included that in my book *How Poets Work* which Seren published in 1996. He had met Dylan in America: "I heard him twice in San Francisco, both times he was quite lushed up." And there was no doubt about the impact he had made: "… the oral tradition which Thomas carried forward when he read was fantastic for many of the local San Francisco poets there … . Dylan Thomas had a very definite effect on the San Francisco renaissance which began in the early 1950s when the Beat Poets arrived from New York – I'm talking about Allen Ginsberg, Gregory Corso, William Burroughs, Jack Kerouac, and others that my little publishing house ended up publishing."

He also said that Allen Ginsberg had made the pilgrimage to Laugharne: "He paid homage to Dylan Thomas, he came to Wales and wrote a long poem of his own at Fern Hill – he happened to write it on LSD, but it's a wonderful long poem … one master recognises another." Indeed.

ॐ

You cannot schedule ghosts or the significant presences of places – Cwmdonkin Park, The Fitzroy, the Chelsea Hotel, Laugharne – but, as Dannie Abse has described his constant preparedness for a poem that may or not come, all you can do is remain open to possibilities and when the moment comes, to recognise it for what it is and what it might be:

Turning

Stopping for salt-marsh lamb
from Eynons – Purveyors of Fine Meats,

on the Blue Boar bridge in the centre of St. Clears,
if you had not turned to double-check the car

that heron priesting the river
would have remained in the blue-grey shade

of overhanging trees, statuesque, dabbing
into the Cynin's shallow, pebbly flow,

an un-witnessed river-lord,
before turning and loping into the air

Laugharne-wards, spreading
his black, grey and white surplice against the sky.

છ

On Poetry Day in 2013 (why on October 3rd; and is not every day a poetry day for fully-formed human beings?) Radio Four's Today programme had Prince Charles reading Dylan's "Fern Hill": what a pleasant surprise at 8.40 in the morning. And read better than some actors on Radio Four's Poetry Please. (Why should it be a pleasant surprise, as Charles's received English is close to the BBC voice of Dylan in his broadcasting prime?) I would guess that the poem addresses several of the Prince's personal agendas – green issues, spiritual revelation through nature and the celebration of creatures on the farm and in the wild. I am assured that it was his choice; he could have read anything. The Prince visited Number 5, Cwmdonkin Drive, as well as the Boat House that year too and is a patron of the 2014 Dylan celebrations. Dylan, the "prince of the apple towns", would have been tickled.

෴

In 1993 I won the Dylan Thomas Prize for Spoken Poetry judged by Dannie Abse and Dylan's daughter Aeronwy. The final event was held on the campus of Loughborough University. The short-listed finalists each read a couple of poems and then a handful of us finished with one extra to decide the winner. I remember that I chose "Incident on a Hospital Train from Calcutta, 1944". Its "incident" was related to me by a mature student on a course which Christine Evans and I ran at the very beginning of the Ty Newydd writing centre in Llanystumdwy. This lady from Newport has admitted from the start that she was not sure that she had anything of interest to make poems. She had served as a Queen Alexandra nurse in the Second World War; she had been at Dunkirk, then India. Christine and I were left open-mouthed at her life and its narrative. She did manage to write a Dunkirk poem by the end of the week; but she insisted that she could never write about the Calcutta train incident, so agreed that I could do that for her.

A British Army hospital train makes it

way up from the city into the hills for coolness; at a stop our nurse, leaning through an open carriage window, was handed a bundle from the platform which turned out to be a sickly and probably infectious baby girl. At the next stop she told her staff to leave the bundle on the platform – "that child would have emptied half our beds …"

The corporal whose arms had gone looked up at me and said, *There was nothing else to do.*
Gangrenous, he died at Murree a week later.
His eyes, I remember, were clear, deep and blue.

Dylan that year was working on propaganda films in "the capital punishment", culminating with *Our Country*, a patriotic filmic context for some of the concerns of his war-time poems. It opens with the words "To begin with the city".

❧

In 2012 and 2013 I re-worked and extended a one-act play which I had written on the Tenby-born painter Nina Hamnett into a full-length play comprising three monologues by Nina, Gwen John and Augustus John. As *Augustus, Gwen and Nina*, this received two amateur performances at the Barry Arts Festival and then in the Tenby Arts Festival in 2013. I have both Nina and Augustus referring to Dylan (Gwen John never met him and would have surely crossed herself and said three Hail Marys if she had).

Augustus, tired and painted-out in his studio in the mid-1950s, says: "Oh, to have died a young genius – Innes, Dylan the syphilitic cherub; Dylan the poor pugilist who punched at me in Carmarthen because I'd tumbled his wench Caitlin Macnamara – buxom Irish girl. What a dancer!"

Nina, the Queen of Fitzrovia, more than surviving in the gloom and pleasures of the London Blitz, says: "We Welsh sticks together in the big city, don't we? Nina, Augustus and Dylan Thomas. Young Dylan's got himself a cosy number in the war films business – hush, hush – 'I'm the Welsh secret weapon against Adolf.' Says he'll try and get me a part. 'I'm a museum piece,' says I. 'I'll dust you off,' says he, 'and make an exhibition of you.'"

She seemed to have forgiven Dylan for his uncomplimentary review of her autobiography *Laughing Torso* in the Western Mail in 1933. Nina, Augustus and Dylan in the war years and afterwards brushed and bobbed and drifted together as part of the flotsam of Fitzrovia – Louis MacNeice and Orwell, the boys from the BBC, Bacon and Freud, the two Roberts, boys who liked boys, Julian Maclaren-Ross, Colin McInnes, the blind-drunk almost-poets and John Heath-Stubbs who really was blind, and really was a poet.

❧

Nina Hamnett was born in Lexton Terrace, the grandest of eighteenth century locations in Tenby with views of Caldey Island and the Gower from all five floors. We have a friend who lives two doors along from Nina's commemorative plaque and it was in her house that the honeymoon scenes of the 2008 Dylan Thomas film *The Edge of Love* were shot. Sienna

Miller and Matthew Rhys as Caitlin and Dylan spend idyllic hours in this "hotel" in 1937 in Cornwall at the beginning of what would prove to be a tempestuous marriage. The money shot was of the pair sitting on a upholstered window seat before the stunning view; except there was no window seat at Lexton Terrace, so the film company built one: "Don't worry, we'll take it away afterwards and put everything back as it was." "No, please leave it there," said our friend. And very comfy it is too.

☙

Andrew Lycett, in his biography of the poet, reports the following conversation:

Augustus John to Dylan Thomas: "All you are is a pot-bellied purveyor of pornographic poetry."

Dylan: "And you, Gus, you are a bearded begetter of bastards."

☙

In recent years we have taken to meeting our old friend and my poetry mentor Dannie Abse for lunch at the Mondello, an Italian family trattoria in Goodge Street in what was Fitzrovia, round the corner from the famous Bertorelli's, frequented by Dylan et al. There are many stories and memories from that most remarkable of Welsh writers, now ninety. Dannie remembers alighting from a bus in Swiss Cottage and encountering Nina Hamnett on the pavement and trying to touch passers-by for a hand-out: "Buy me a drink, dearie, my fucking cat is dead."

It cost him half a crown: she swigged down her gin and tonic and left him alone in the pub with his desultory half-pint. Shortly after Dylan's death Dannie wrote an elegy for him:

look up in surprise, in a hurt public house
or in a rain-blown street, and see how
no fat ghost but a quotation cries.

And once the young doctor met Dylan Thomas, in a pub, of course. As in awe of Dylan as I would be later of Vernon Watkins, Dannie was pretty tongue-tied, but mentioned his Swansea cousin, the painter Leo Solomon. Dylan must have known this contemporary, but offered no response. When Dannie left, "Goodbye Mr Thomas," he said. "Goodbye, Mr Solomon," Dylan replied.

Dylan's poetry had been such powerful force in the years before and after the war that you were either of or against his party. Dannie's first collection was accepted by Hutchinson while he was still a medical student in London, but published a couple of years later in 1948. *After Every Green Thing* was a false start for a poet who might be taken for a Movement fellow-traveller before finding his own path through realism and allusion, his own remarkable voice. As Vernon Watkins observed: "Like Hopkins, he always seemed to me a poet whom it was fatal to copy." In mid-century British poetics Dylan was the mountain you had either to climb or bypass, tunnelling through him left you in the dark. In fact, the post-war, post-Dylan years would see a move to distance contemporary writing from the influence of Dylan Thomas; Kingsley Amis's satires on the Swansea poet in works such as *That Uncertain Feeling* and *The Old Devils* may have contributed to the reluctance of those at the university in that town to embrace their most famous writer.

❧

On the wall above the door to my study I have a framed and double-sided copy of the lithograph "The Force that Through the Green Fuse Drives the Flower", the centre-spread from *Poetry London* Vol. 3 No. 2, 1945, probably

Ceri Richards's first public response to Dylan's poetry: it marks my place and keeps me in my place.

৩

After the Ceri Richards retrospective at the Glynn Vivian Gallery in Swansea in 2003 Margaret and I went for a meal afterwards in The Slow Boat Chinese restaurant on High Street with Richard Burns and Dylan's daughter Aeronwy Thomas. Aeronwy was charming, while Richard, released from his efforts at the exhibition, drank steadily and, as always, was erudite and garrulous.

Ceri Richards's work changed gear into a metaphorical intensity under the influence of Dylan's poetry. Richard Burns has argued persuasively that even the magisterial late work of the "Drowned Cathedral" series owes its inspiration to the poems: in "The Ballad of the Long-Legged Bait" – "Floated the lost cathedral / Chimes of the rocked buoys ... " Dylan's name has its origin in the *Mabinogion* where Dylan Eil Ton, Second Son of the Wave, as soon as he came to the sea "received the sea's nature". Dylan's "lovely, ugly town" is a port, a bay, neck-laced by the sea, "the infant-bearing sea" and Dylan Thomas's poetry surely added to "the sea's nature". Certainly, Ceri Richards's *La Cathedrale Engloutie* series is the most notable of his work (shown at the 1962 Venice Biennale) and these are some of the finest paintings from the 1960s in these islands.

The previous year I had met Richard Burns off the London train at Cardiff for a poetry reading at my university and we had a coffee in a quiet café in the Morgan Arcade. We talked of the research he had done for his fascinating book *Ceri Richards and Dylan Thomas: Keys to Transformation*. At one point he seemed to gaze fixedly over my shoulder into the sky; I'm pressing him a bit hard after his long journey from Cambridge, I thought. Then Richard returned to fix his gaze on me and began to speak, not recite, speak, "Fern Hill". The whole poem, celebrating the words, every one of them.

৽৩

I only ever attended one Dylan Thomas poetry reading: for in his performance of "Return Journey and other Works" the actor Bob Kingdom *became* Thomas. In the Sherman Theatre in Cardiff in 1990 you did not even have to close your eyes to believe that it was Thomas, for Kingdom's body and that of the later, bloated and bulb-nosed poet merged; and the voice was perfect Swansea BBC, perfect for the 1953 American tours.

Some twenty years later I was invited to the Dylan Thomas house at Number 5, Cwmdonkin Avenue, to contribute to a recording about Dylan and his work for a podcast production. Around the scullery table were biographer Andrew Lycett, poet Peter Thabbit-Jones, actor and Richard Burton's nephew Guy Masterson and Bob Kingdom. After we'd done our stuff I cornered Bob and gushed at him like a fan, which is what I am. Time waits for no man – sizzled poet or ageing actor – but for decades on stages around the world, lauded by Eric Clapton, no less, at very special moments, the lamented poet and the talented actor seemed to occupy the same moment, the same body, on the same stage.

❦

In the summer of 1995 we flew to the States to see our son Gareth who was at the University of Massachusetts for his American Studies year abroad from Swansea University. The head of art at UMASS, our friend Hanlyn Davies from Gorseinon, accompanied Gareth to meet us off the bus. Gareth told us that he'd had a phone message for me: Glyn Jones had died earlier that day.

I had known Glyn for some years. He had helped me polish my *Writers of Wales* book on Dannie Abse; he had agreed to be interviewed by my colleague Mike Parnell and me as part of the *Fiction Writers of Wales* series of videos I had produced at the university; he had donated manuscripts to our Welsh Writing in English Centre on the campus. In my study I have a framed photo of Glyn and John Ormond and Jean Henderson and me sitting on a bench in Whitchurch dedicated to the poet John Tripp, Jean's friend, who had died in 1986.

I visited Glyn many times at his home on Manor Way in Whitchurch. He had books signed by Dylan, including a copy of *Eighteen Poems* which Dylan had given him in London on its publication in 1934, and a collection of letters from him over a number of years. Glyn was a principled, Christian gentleman who had in 1939 declared himself a pacifist and suffered the sack from his teaching post and considerable hardship when he was too old for conscription and could have kept his head down for the duration. Meanwhile, Dylan had frantically pulled every string and almost exhausted his wit in avoiding conscription: the army would eventually dismiss him as unfit in any case.

Glyn first met Dylan in 1934 after writing to him a letter of admiration for two poems he'd read in the *Adelphi* magazine. Dylan was almost ten years younger than the young Cardiff school master: Glyn later described him as "angelic and tremendously endearing ... wearing a black polo-necked sweater and a pair of shabby grey trousers, the sort of intellectual mufti of the thirties".

Glyn Jones and Dylan Thomas shared the castled village of Llanstephan in their background: the graves of their relatives are in the burial ground of Capel Newydd, Llanybri, above the village. In his important survey of writing in Wales *The Dragon has Two Tongues*, published in 1968, Glyn tells of the two writers meeting in Llanstephan before the war and walking over the Parc yr Arglwydd headland to the estuary at Laugharne. They rang the bell to summon the ferryman who rowed them across past the Boat House and below the castle to the small town and afternoon tea in Brown's Hotel.

Before returning they walked up to the church of St Martin's and the graveyard where Dylan has rested since 1953.

The last time I saw Glyn was when I visited him in his sick-bed in the house in Manor Way, just two days before we flew off to America. He'd had an arm amputated a couple of years before, but the cancer was a lit fuse in his green flower.

We talked of Wales, and friends
and literature,
what was left to write.
I held his left hand
worn as ninety-year-old leather
and tried not to look
at the stump of his other
phantomed in his folded pyjama sleeve.
His eyes were empty and wet.
His hand, light as a feather,
gripped mine like a child's
when I rose to leave.

When asked if he believed in God
"Often," he said.

John Ormond, sitting next to Glyn on that
John Tripp bench in Whitchurch some ten
years before, has his legs crossed and wears a
jaunty cap, a bit like Lenin on his day off. John
Ormond Thomas was an undergraduate at
Swansea in its early days. He went on to work
for the prestigious news magazine *Picture Post*
and then made films on writers and artists for
the BBC in Cardiff, including Dylan, Vernon
and Ceri Richards. It was a golden age for the
BBC in Cardiff and John was given his head:
every film he made in that series was a classic.
Despite, or because of, Vernon Watkins's advice
the undergraduate poet had developed into
one of the more significant figures in poetry in
Wales after the war.

John Ormond, along with the composer
Dan Jones, was closely involved in attempting
to see that Dylan's funeral went smoothly in
Laugharne; after the coffin had been brought
back from the liner *SS United States*, docked at
Southampton, by Ebbie Williams, landlord of
Brown's Hotel, there were problems. Dylan's

open casket was propped on chairs in front of the bookcase in his mother's house, the Pelican, in the town a short walk from the Boat House. Dan Jones later described the scene: "[Dylan's] face was plastered with cosmetics, forehead and skin covered with pancake make-up, cheeks heavily rouged, mouth vividly lip-sticked; even the most brassy tart would not have ventured onto the streets in such a get-up." Despite their efforts the funeral turned "into a sort of farcical nightmare ... the drinking, the violence, the sex ..."

Two years before that photograph of the bench in Whitchurch I had included two poems by Glyn Jones in the *Wales/America Portfolio of Poems and Prints*, produced by Professor Fred Jones in Western Illinois, each poem rendered by calligraphy and illuminated by the artist Jonah Jones. Glyn had suggested that I invite John Ormond, but John argued that as there was to be no fee it was against his principle that poets should always be paid for their work. This was not because he needed the money, but that others might. The portfolio appeared with Welsh poets Euros Bowen, Gwyn Thomas and Bobi Jones as well as myself, Glyn Jones, Dannie Abse and Gillian Clarke; each poem was designed and illuminated by Jonah Jones. The print-makers included Hanlyn Davies and Fred Jones himself. Each contributor received a large and beautifully produced portfolio. John missed the opportunity to add that to his fine art collection with Kyffin Williams and Ceri Richards; we missed the opportunity to include a fine poet in our project.

Incidentally, although they knew each other well, the only letter to John Ormond from Dylan in the 1,000-plus page *The Collected Letters* is from late in December, 1947: "What about my cheque? Can you hasten it up? I'm dead broke after a loud, wet Christmas, and relying on Picture Post. Do your best – *as soon as possible*. URGENT. See you, I hope, in London sometime next week. Yours, Dylan."

⁓

On St David's Day 1982 in Westminster Abbey a commemorative floor slab for Dylan Thomas was unveiled in Poets' Corner. It is of Penrhyn green slate with the carved words of dedication and the last lines of "Fern Hill" incised by Jonah Jones. He is shown working on the lettering in John Ormond's Dylan film for the BBC. The memorial was put in place largely due to the influence of President Jimmy Carter who was surprised to see one of his most admired poets absent from the Abbey: "You put him in here. And I will pray for him."

I knew Jonah well, from his work on the Poems and Prints Portfolio and in his later years when he and Judith lived in Cardiff. Jonah learned much of his craft in the Eric Gill workshops after the war and was also commissioned to make the Abbey's commemoration to Lloyd George. I interviewed Jonah for the *Welsh Artists Talking* book and he told me that reading a Dylan Thomas story in *The Listener*, specifically the John Petts drawing of the Swansea Strand which illustrated it, determined him to locate Petts in the army, which meant volunteering for the Parachute Regiment, a decision made all the more impressive as Jonah had declared himself a conscientious objector and served in the Paras as an unarmed medic. He parachuted into France and followed in the pursuit of the retreating German army, parachuting again at Wesel on the Rhine. When his unit reached Belsen, he said, his pacifism was shaken. He told me, "Looking back, I find the position untenable."

Dylan's position was tenable and determined: he did not want to go and saw himself as irrelevant to the cause. A few days after war had been declared he wrote: "The Army Medical Corps is presumably admirable, but I don't want to help – even in a most inefficient way – to patch poor buggers up to send them out again into quick insanity and bullets." A few weeks later he wrote: "My only war joke is that I have been thinking of volunteering as a small tank." Though a week before Christmas that year he took part in an entertainment in Laugharne to raise money for the Red Cross which the novelist Richard Hughes's wife Frances had organised: Dylan acted in a short farce written by Ernest Goodwin, while the second item on the bill was "Tap dance by Mrs D Thomas."

The irony was that it was Dylan who would produce the finest of all the poems written in the war: "A Refusal to Mourn the Death, by Fire, of a Child in London"

⁓

In 1990 I published *How to Study Modern Poetry*, a study guide in a series for Macmillan. Taking three poems from each of the post-war decades I critiqued them in a systematic way as a means to encourage a common-sense approach by students and to offer a safe set of working principles. In the chapter on the 1940s and 1950s I included Dylan's "A Refusal to Mourn the Death, by Fire, of a Child in London". The first thirteen lines, of course, are one unpunctuated sentence. It shouldn't work, but it is a marvellous and moving piece of affirmative rhetoric. It ends – "After the first death there is no other." And that, despite Vernon Watkins's conviction that Dylan was a Christian poet, is beautifully ambiguous, triumphantly ambiguous. In 2007 I chose that line as the title of my anthology of writing about "Wales and war in the twentieth century".

In January 1998, I visited one of the Kardomah Boys, Alfred Janes, in his house in Dulwich to record an interview with him for my book *Welsh Artists Talking*. Then I gave an appreciation of the man at the Society of Arts in London as part of the celebrations after his death the following year.

In 1934 Dylan and Fred Janes had rented rooms in London directly underneath another Swansea painter, Mervyn Levy. "[Dylan] would sit in his overcoat in bed with that pork-pie hat and write poetry while I painted in the other corner."

While they lived in Redcliffe Gardens, Fred painted a portrait of the young poet which is now in the National Museum of Wales collection. Dylan was not an easy sitter, he was "in and out like a cat in a tripe shop," Fred told me. On leave during the war, he frequently met Dylan in the Fitzroy Tavern, often with Nina Hamnett as part of the furniture.

In 1953 it was Fred and Mary Janes who drove the painter Ceri Richards down to the

Boat House to visit the poet he so admired. They got on famously and there was talk of Dylan working on a project with Ceri; then Caitlin returned and a row broke out at which point Ceri and the Janeses left. Fred told me that he considered Ceri Richards "the most creative and inventive painter of this century." Dylan's father had taught Fred English at Swansea Grammar School: Mary Janes told me that, "[Dylan's father] had no children's books, so he read Shakespeare and the classics to him."

Fred Janes was a lovely man, a trained and dedicated artist, so dedicated in fact that Dylan, enquiring about their Kardomah artist friend asked in a letter to Vernon Watkins in 1946: "How is that blizzardly painter, that lightning artist, that prodigal canvas-stacker? Has he reached the next finbone of the fish he was dashing off before the war?" Fred's legendary lack of speed in completing oil paintings was belied when he took me upstairs to the bedroom where he kept his work: the room was full of the paintings and constructions he'd made in the decades following his exposure to the exhibition of the American Abstract Impressionism in London in 1956: the blizzard had swept him up in its path.

❧

At the start of Dylan's centenary year the National Museum of Wales in Cardiff put on a large exhibition of Peter Blake's works based on *Under Milk Wood*: the notable pop artist and creator of the Beatles' *Sergeant Pepper's Lonely Hearts Club Band* album cover had heard the radio broadcast when a student in the Royal College; he had been fascinated by Dylan's play for decades and some years back he started a series of small watercolours depicting scenes from Llareggub. By 2014 those had expanded over the decades to include many more works – collages and, most remarkably, a project to complete pencil drawings of every character appearing or even mentioned in the play. Homage indeed, to stand alongside the Stan Tracey jazz suite and the proposed *Under Milk Wood* opera by John Metcalfe.

We attended a discussion at the Museum with Sir Peter and the Dylan book expert Jeff Towns and a few weeks later I was invited to give a lunch-time talk there on Dylan and the artists, essentially, the core of this little book. My problem with the Blake exhibition was that after the initial water-colours and the intriguingly surreal collages, when I reached the character sketch section – some 60 small works on the far wall – I encountered Captain Cat depicted as the aviator Tommy Sopwith, Rosie Probert unmistakably Elizabeth Taylor then the Second Voice played by Humphrey Bogart. There followed (quite recognisably, because I had met and worked with both ladies) Beryl Bainbridge and Margaret Atwood. Who on earth in the play were they supposed to be?

Of course, Dylan – like many other significant writers – has inspired visual artists, notably Ceri Richards and John Petts, and more recently in Wales John Selway and Robert Alwyn Hughes. I have three depictions of the Boat House in my collection – by Ray Howard-Jones, John Petts and John T. Freeman. In 2003 the

Swansea Print Workshop produced a portfolio of twelve new prints interpreting "Especially When the October Wind", including one by my friend and colleague Ceri Thomas; there will, no doubt, be others.

Interesting work this paying *homage*: how much of one's own baggage may one load onto to the subject of the *homage*? Dear Reader, you must judge for yourself. In mitigation may I point out that the present work gives its honest intent in the title; read it as you may:

My Life: with Dylan Thomas.
My Life ... with Dylan Thomas.
My Life. With Dylan Thomas.
My Life with: Dylan Thomas.

ഩ

I've been a guest writer at Tenby Arts Club several times over the years. What is always mentioned is the fact that it was at the Arts Club in early October 1953 that Dylan first read from and performed much of the final version of *Under Milk Wood* just before his fateful last trip to America. My old deputy headmaster at Greenhill School, Bill Davies, was there and assured me of this. So too was the poet Raymond Garlick whose poem commemorating the evening I included in my 1989 anthology *The Poetry of Pembrokeshire*:

… The scene was set
for speech, and nervously he stirred and spoke –
shuffling the pack of papers on his knee
at random drew one, stared and woke
into awareness …

… It was October, the month of birthdays.
The saga was nearly ended.

What is also well remembered is that Dylan spent so long in The Coach and Horses in Upper Frog Street – "the oldest public house within the town walls" – that they had trouble getting him home. A sign outside the pub now claims that the poet left his copy of *Under Milk Wood* there and had to rush back from Tenby station to retrieve it before flying off to the USA again.

The publisher and BBC producer Douglas Cleverdon records that the following week in London Dylan again lost the script, this time in a Soho pub; luckily Cleverdon had arranged for his secretary at the Beeb to run off stencilled copies, three of which Dylan then had with him for the flight to New York. After completing two readings in New York and having added another page to the play's ending, Dylan collapsed and was taken to hospital on November 5th.

ↁ

One of the many guests I invited to the Creative Writing masters course at university was a friend of Dannie Abse's the eminent American poet Stanley Moss. Decades before, as a young poet working in publishing in New York, Stanley was familiar with Thomas's work and reputation; recognising him in a bar in Greenwich Village he struck up a conversation. Dylan confided that he drank simply "… because I don't do anything really useful." Dylan spent time in Howard's apartment and once, in a taxi with Stanley as audience, Dylan did a fine impression of God receiving T.S. Eliot into heaven. Dylan could be a dangerous drunk, but also a most entertaining drunk.

In 1953 Stanley mourned the loss of his Welsh poet friend:

In this pit
The word is my bread,
I pass the word
And let the others know.

Stanley had also known Dr. Feltenstein, who clearly indicated to him that he had, in fact, given Dylan an injection of morphine. Most medics and biographers now agree that it was that drug which caused his death.

Also in that year Alassandro Contini-Bonacossi died; he was an art collector who had some of the finest examples of Old Masters in private hands. Stanley Moss, urbane, witty and a fine linguist, became the art dealer and agent who placed the Italian's works by Goya, Tiepolo, Zurbaran and Piero de la Francesca in some of the world's great public art collections.

In *The New Yorker* back in September last year Stanley, published a new poem – in his eighty-eighth year to heaven, sixty years after Dylan's death.

❧

In the autumn of 1978 Margaret and I arranged for friends to look after our two young children and had a weekend on the Gower: I had won the *Western Mail's* Dylan Thomas Prize for Poetry and some bright spark had put together sponsorship so that the prize was not money, but a "gourmet weekend on the Gower". We could only manage to be away for one night so negotiated a deal whereby we had dinner at very expensive French restaurant off the Mumbles Road and a night at the Osborne Hotel in Langland Bay, which was then a fine place – we had Dublin Bay prawns for breakfast. We were chauffeured to and from the hotel in a car so large and grand that it may well have been a Bentley. The competition was judged by Roland Mathias and a new poet Sheenagh Pugh, who some fifteen years later I appointed to teach with us at the university.

My winning poem was one of those written earlier that year at the time of my father's death. So we fed off death, as it were. At the posh restaurant to accompany our steaks we ordered the most expensive bottle of red on the wine list. Whatever it was, it was so rich and full-bodied that we could not finish it. The Dylan Thomas Prize for Poetry was not honoured in its alcohol consumption then.

❧

My father's funeral had been at the crematorium in Narberth in August in 1978. Avoiding a conventional eulogy I chose to read "Do Not Go Gentle into that Good Night". I think that it was more to do with being able to stay cool and professional performing someone else's words; I certainly could not have read one from the series of poems I was working on during his diagnosis, treatment and decline. Thomas's great poem got me out of a spot, resolved a dilemma. How often must that great rhetorical poem have worked to great effect?

ɔ

The Kardomah coffee house which housed in its upstairs room the roaring boys – Dylan, Fred Janes, Dan Jones – had been converted from the Congregationalist Church in which Dylan's parents had been married in December 1903 (his mother probably pregnant with his sister Nancy). That part of the narrative holds the key for much that was to characterise the changes in twentieth century Wales. I recently discovered that Beatrice Mary Barrah, my grandmother from a Pembrokeshire farming family, and Jim Curtis, the railway worker from Newbury, were married in 1918 and were living in Johnstown where Dylan's grandparents had their house. My father was born just seven months later: marriages could be hastily arranged in those days.

West Wales and the Great Western Railway combined in both our families. Dylan's grandfather, like mine, left a farm background to work as a guard on God's Wonderful Railway based at the large engine sheds and terminal at Carmarthen. Our backgrounds both reflected that widespread move from west Wales farming to industry that shaped modern Wales.

❧

I'm over in Aberystwyth for a poetry reading and we are guests of the poet Matthew Francis and his wife Creina in the village of Llanon. We've been down to the pebbly coast of the Cardigan on previous visits but this time after breakfast they take us for a walk up a path inland following river Peris. It's part of what is now marketed as the Dylan Thomas Trail. Matthew tells us that Dylan walked up this rough path following the Peris to visit friends in an old farmhouse, now occupied by folk who have an abandoned Peugeot as a shed and who grow their own.

The local writer David Thomas has argued forcefully that *Under Milk Wood* is rooted more firmly in Ceredigion and New Quay than Carmarthenshire and Laugharne. Certainly, Dylan had family connections here and when he was working on propaganda films in London during the war Catlin stayed in New Quay and they received film production people at their rented bungalow Majoda above New Quay. It was here that the infamous William Killick grenade and Sten gun attack took place in 1945.

Inland is the Aeron Valley where Aeronwy may have been conceived and after which she was named. Also in the locality is Plas Llanina where Lord Howard de Walden allowed Dylan to use the apple house as a study. Not to mention Geoffrey Faber's house Tyglyn Aeron where T.S. Eliot stayed regularly before the war.

On our January walk the river is a brown torrent and one of its tributaries blocks our path. Tumbling water is the only sound, the colours are a dark and mossy green; but we know that through the trees and over the hill are the rich, rolling Ceredigion fields forever rendered into the Garden of Eden by the painter John Elwyn. This is a country where "The Salt is on the briar-rose, / The fog is in the fir trees." Could not this land of the early saints and the struggle for survival just as well have been a location for one of the *Four Quartets*?

Rain forces us to return to Lanon and their remarkable house, one of several built there by retired Captain Cats in the nineteenth century. Matthew signs a copy of his new Faber collection for us. In the first poem his man in the wind sails for that west moon pulled by a flight of geese – "Wingbeat by wingbeat we clambered up the sky."

There is always poetry in the air in Ceredigion, as Dylan well knew.

ε⁄ͻ

When I visited Vernon Watkins's widow, Gwen, some years back in my research on Ceri Richards, of course she had many memories of both Dylan and Ceri. She had worked at Bletchley Park, the code-breaking centre during the war and had met her future husband there; when I asked about Vernon she said that he'd been a sergeant in the RAF Police, "Though I don't think he ever arrested anyone." Was that because he too was a code-breaker? I thought later.

Gwen was at that point still maintaining the silence that was mandatory for those who had served at Bletchley Park. Of course, Vernon was involved in the code work at Bletchley Park; he'd been on RAF police duties earlier: a man who'd done a year of French and German at Cambridge, who at that time was translating the poems of Heinrich Heine, would he really have been confined to perimeter fence duties? More recently, Gwen Watkins's fascinating book about their time at Bletchley, makes clear that they were both employed in intelligence work, along with another Kardomah boy Dan

Jones, who lived in a local farmhouse, well-fed and in some style. Dan Jones was commissioned as captain, while Vernon stumbled, literally, over the more practical demands of his officer assessment and, in any case, declared that he was happy to remain a sergeant as the table tennis standard at Bletchley was much higher with fellow NCOs, one of whom was the current English champion. While Dylan was in London composing satirical dubbings of speeches by the Nazi leaders, his Swansea friends were de-coding their military orders.

☙

It is tempting to surmise that Bletchley, with its unique assemblage of the brainy, the quirky and the unconventional in behaviour and character traits, could have made use of a brain whose powers of association, the ordering of words in patterns, the assembling of codes through metaphor, sounds and allusions – Dylan's. Might he have been better used in such a place than doing pretty low-level propaganda film work? During his time at Bletchley Dan could pop down into London on leave and did meet with Dylan in the pubs.

In his memoir *My Friend Dylan Thomas* Dan implies not: "The light of Dylan's interest and attention was narrowly focussed on a single area, and everything around this was shrouded in darkness. All systematic studies based on observation, calculation or conjecture were abandoned to this outer darkness."

The central and crucial mind at work at Bletchley Park was, of course, Alan Turing. He developed the means by which the Enigma codes could be broken and continued to pioneer computer research after the war. In 1986 we saw the play about his life and tragic end on stage in the West End, with Derek Jacobi as Turing. Prosecuted for homosexual practices in 1952, he chose to be chemically castrated rather than be imprisoned. He died some months after Dylan Thomas by eating an apple laced with cyanide. A black apple, indeed. At the end of 2013, when I was writing this, Alan Turing was finally "pardoned by the Queen".

❧

Every time we drive down to our house in Lydstep we stop in Carmarthen and park in that large car-park where my junior school Pentrepoeth had stood, or sometimes in the multi-storey next to the new Debenham's. My parents had pulled some strings to get me into that school; I should have gone to The Model School off Catherine Street, where my father and uncle had gone and where Dylan's father DJ Thomas had been taught before his successful entry to the University of Aberystwyth.

From the top floor of Debenham's car-park I can look down on Pentrefelin Street and the back garden of the house where I was born. Next-door-but-one and also a few doors further along were two families of coracle fishermen, one called the Thomas Dwr. They would have been the background characters as Dylan's Grandpa was asked:

" 'And what do you think you are doing on Carmarthen bridge in the middle of the afternoon … with your best waistcoat and your old hat?'

Grandpa did not answer, but inclined his

face to the river wind, so that his beard was set dancing and wagging as though he talked, and watched the coracle men move, like turtles, on the shore. 'I am going to Llangadock to be buried.' And he watched the coracle shells slip into the water lightly, and the gulls complain over the fish-filled water ...' There's no sense in lying dead in Llanstephan.'"

On a fine autumn day in 1995 we attended a brief ceremony of the interment of Glyn Jones's ashes in the church of St. Stephen on the Towy estuary; Glyn was a deeply serious man with an irrepressible twinkling humour; he saw every sense in lying dead in Llanstephan and was smiling over us that day.

❧

On our journeys to Pembrokeshire we invariably stop for coffee in the first-floor Café Revive of M&S in Carmarthen. Looking out of the window at the pedestrianised street with its Boots and Clarks shoe shop I can't help but see the ghost of Nelson's Garage where my father worked after the war and through the decade of the 1950s. The other side of the street behind the bland and uniform retail units, in a lane now gone, he had his workshop where my mother and I would sometimes visit; he'd be there with dismantled electric car parts, repaired not simply discarded and replaced in those days, and the Sorcerers' sinister large glass containers of battery acid with their acrid and biting tang. Oh, and always an unconscious Woodbine at his lips. This workshop was on Shaw's Lane close to The Stag's Head and the Nelson Hotel; it may well have been on the spot where the Ladbroke's Bookies is now. Just up Lammas Street at the end of the lane is The Boar's Head regularly frequented (as were many of the town's myriad pubs) by Dylan on his way from Laugharne to the rest of the world. Lammas Street which in "A Visit to Grandpa's" is where the young Dylan and his Grandpa's neighbours "rattled down" in their search for the old man, gone missing from Llanstephan. At The Boar's Head before the war Augustus John had punched Dylan and left him on the road while he drove off with Caitlin to bed her in Laugharne. On the eighth of October, 1953, it was at The Whore's Bed, as he re-named the hotel, that Dylan took his last drink in west Wales before catching the train to London and the plane to New York.

From my father's work-shop on our way back home to Pentrefelin Street we'd make our way up Lammas Street towards Brian the Butcher's whose plump breasts, splayed legs and firm sausages were carefully weighted and wrapped as *double entendres*.

It is a sunny autumn day with candy floss clouds and not a hint of rain from the west. As we pass the Boar's Head Hotel a man emerges, half-stumbling, loudly proclaiming in mid-sentence, "... Carmarthen, Carmarthen, on my pennyfarthen'..." and my mother takes my hand more firmly and pulls me a little too quickly down the street.

තු

The last long poem on which Dylan Thomas worked was to be "In Country Sleep", a five-part sequence which included the title poem, "Over Sir John's Hill" and "In the White Giant's Thigh". Vernon Watkins recovered the draft of this unfinished poem and, remarkably, added another five verses of five lines to run on from the last line of Dylan's draft: it is somewhere between a tour de force and a pastiche of his dead friend.

The last line that Dylan had written was –

Young Aesop fabling by the coracled Towy ...

And that seems to me as good a place as any to finish the thing.